## ACKNOWLEDGEMENTS

Many thanks to Mary Jo for helping me organize all of the Lost Quotes, to Fleck and Bonno for helping me create the cover, and to Maury "Han" Harris for helping me find some of the Lost Quotes and pushing me on this historic project.

## DEDICATION

To all those who have been quoted . . .

# INTRODUCTION

Throughout History, ancient and recent, many people have been quoted saying all kinds of things. Well, some of those quotes were lost!

# LOST QUOTES

## JOHN MARKS

## Cover illustrated by Chris Bonno
## Cover designed by Mike Fleckenstein

TORANAGA PRESS
Washington, D.C.

Published by
TORANAGA PRESS
Washington, D.C.

Library of Congress Cataloging-in-Publication Data
Marks, John, 1994
Lost Quotes/by John Marks
ISBN 0-9642648-0-3

Printed in the United States of America

1st printing, 1994

Willard Press, Manassas, Virginia
Cover illustrated by Chris Bonno. Cover designed by Mike Fleckenstein

**"Forgive me, Queen, but I don't like the names the Nina, the Pinta, and the Santa Maria. How about just Boat #1, Boat #2, and Boat #3?"**

*-Columbus talking to Queen Isabella*

---

**"What do you mean you've not yet begun to rake your yard?."**

*-John Paul Jones's neighbor*

"You know, if you put an 'L' on the end of NASA, it would spell nasal."

-Dan Quayle

"Forget taking Persia, I say we dance!"

-Alexander the Great

**"Personally, I would like to paint the White House a nice mauve color!"**

*-Mrs. Grover Cleveland*

---

**"Look!  The edge of the planet!, . . . Just kiddin'."**

*-Columbus*

**"You forgot the peanuts?"**

*-Orville to Wilbur Wright before their first flight*

**"What do you mean you want a chase scene?"**

*-Karl Marx talking to his editor about Das Kapital*

**"What purpose can this serve except to be a non-functional physical tribute to oppression of the masses through hard labor?"**

*-Two slaves discussing the pyramids*

---

**"Man, I'm freezin' my butt off."**

*-Admiral Peary at the South Pole*

"Man, I can't believe I cut my ear off."

*-Van Gogh, the next day*

"I shall return. . . . now do you spell this Island with an 'F' or a 'Ph'?"

*-MacArthur*

"So, there I am riding and slashing through a band of angry heretics, when all of a sudden I get this burning, itching feeling."

-Sir Lancelot talking to his doctor

"In the name of God, St. George, St. Michael, I knight thee, . . . Oh, I'm sorry, I seem to have cut your neck."

-King Richard knighting his fight knight

"Hey, Baby, give me a kiss, . . . What's your problem?"

*-Senator Packwood*

---

"Dan, could you please wait outside, I'm talking to the National Security Council."

*-Bush talking to Quayle*

**"I keep seeing snow."**

*-Napoleon's psychic right before he went into Russia*

**"I keep seeing Indians."**

*-Custer's psychic*

"I keep seeing rope."

-Mussolini's psychic

"Does triangulation mean anything to you?"

-JFK's psychic

**"Moses, for petesake, it's been forty years, will you please pull over and ask someone."**

*-Mrs. Moses*

---

**"He's gonna make the Red Sea part? Moses?  The same guy with the burning bush story?"**

*-Slave following Moses*

11

"You think you're going to make a name for yourself by writing songs?"

*-Francis Scott Key's mother*

---

"Honey, please leave the dog alone and quit playing with that doorbell."

*-Pavlov's mother*

"Leave me alone, I'm meditating."

*-Buddha*

"Sure is quiet out here!"

*-Thoreau at Walden Pond*

13

"So, you see the mind of man is, . . . are you people getting this at all?"

*-Socrates*

---

"When I say put your pencils down, I mean put your pencils down."

*-Aristotle in front of his class at the end of a test*

"If one more person asks me, 'When are we going to fight the Persians?, When are we going to fight the Persians?', then we're not going to fight the Persians!"

*-Alexander the Great*

"Ooooooooooooooh, Ooooooooooooooooh, I've got a cramp in my leg."

*-Sitting Bull*

"Albert, do you have any theories on why the relatives keep coming to visit?"

*-Einstein's father*

"How many times do I have to tell you? Stay away from those train tracks!"

*-Doppler's mother*

**"Men, I'm going to have to put my foot down.  No more coffee breaks. We're vikings!"**

*-Lief Ericson*

**"So what's your problem?"**

*-Freud talking to a patient on a busy day*

**"Untie yourself and come to dinner."**

*-Houdini's mother*

**"Yea, that noose is a little tight."**

*-Mussolini*

**"I'm assuming we'll have a bridge built connecting Gaza with Jericho!"**

*-Yasser Arafat*

**"Now, again, Arafat is the one with the towel thing on his head, right?"**

*-Gore to Clinton before the Peace Treaty signing ceremony*

"... So I took my sword and stabbed him right in the throat. You should of seen the look on his face. More wine for everyone. Then there was the time I .."

*-Kublai Khan telling war stories*

"You're not going to light that are you?"

*-Joan of Arc at the stake*

20

**"Did you go to Florida?"**

*-Columbus' neighbor*

**"You know what I miss the most since I've been in seclusion?  Putt Putt!"**

*-Salman Rushdie*

"Oh great, the Pacific Ocean.  I was just getting into a rhythm."

*-Lewis to Clark*

"Bolivia?  Now that's in South America, right?"

*-Dan Quayle*

**"Hey, cancel the hemlock, how about just a frozen Pina Colada?"**

*-Socrates talking to a bartender at a party*

- - - - - - - - - - - - - - - - - - - - - - - - - - - - - - - - - - - - - - - - - - - - - - - - - - - - - - - - - - - - - - - - - - - - - - - - - - - -

**"Round?  I've always felt the planet was oblong."**

*-Columbus' neighbor*

**"Honey, he's not a garden snake, he's a serpent, and why did you invite him to dinner?"**

*-Adam to Eve*

---

**"Really a shame, good woman like that!"**

*-Two soldiers watching Joan of Arc burn at the stake*

**"You're as young as you feel!"**

*-Methuselah the day before he died*

---

**"Pablo, quit distorting your face.  It'll get stuck like that."**

*-Picasso's mother talking to young Pablo*

"I don't know, Doc.  All she does is work on that darned flag.  Of course, I feel neglected."

*-The husband of Betsy Ross*

"There goes Columbus, says he discovered the new world, won't let you forget it either."

*-Some guy who knew Columbus*

**"Why did Hess buy a kilt?"**

*-Hitler looking at his bills*

---

**"The consciousness of man is a mass agreed upon result of, . . . Excuse me, are you finished with that piece of pie?"**

*-Buddha pontificating at a restaurant*

**"You had to go and tell everyone we're not the center of the universe."**

*-Mrs. Copernicus*

---

**"How long til we get to the new world? Five minutes less than the last time you asked me."**

*-Columbus to first mate*

28

"Hess went to Scotland!  Uh Oh!"

*-Hitler*

"Pharoah, Schmaroah, he can't tell us what to do!"

*-Moses*

**"It's not a tetrahedron, it's a tedrahedron."**

*-Two Egyptian slaves arguing about the shape of the Pyramids*

---

**"Nobody trusts me anymore."**

*-Benedict Arnold*

**"Of course, my ultimate goal is track lighting."**

*-Edison*

**"I have no idea where I am!"**

*-Amelia Earhart*

"It says in Revelations chapter, . . .
uh chapter, . . . uh, hey, Tony, what
chapter was that locust thing?"

-The Pope in 1455

"Columbus just found out the earth isn't
flat.  It's round.  All those flat globes we
just made are worthless!"

-Gino Luchese, the largest maker
of flat globes in Europe in 1492

**"So I shaved by head bald, Mom, what do you think?"**

*-Buddha talking to his mother*

---

**"Get your ape hands off me!"**

*-A drunk Charles Darwin*

"Hold on, son, that's not how you do a card trick."

*-Merlin's father*

---

"It's the new world, we've discovered the new world, . . . wait, who are those people on the beach?"

*-Columbus*

**"Okay, men, on the count of three, we charge the castle. Now don't forget, there is a moat there, and no pushing."**

-*King Richard before a battle*

**"You know, guys, I never really liked Hitler. I was just playing the game, waiting for the right moment to take him out. Can you let me go?"**

-*Nazi criminal Field Marshal Wilhelm Keitel's last words before being hung for war crimes in Nuremburg*

**"Will you call me when you get there to let me know you're safe?"**

*-Mrs. Neil Armstrong before his historical flight to the moon*

---

**"I don't care what anybody says.  No snow ice cream tonight!"**

*-Admiral Peary on the way to the South Pole*

**"Hey, how ya doin', I'm Jonas Salk. I invented the polio vaccine. Can I buy you a drink?"**

*-Dr. Salk hitting on a woman at a bar*

**"Oh boy, another snorkel, thanks, Dad."**

*-Jacque Cousteau's son opening a present on his birthday*

"Okay, men, good luck.  I think we can defeat the enemy.  Remember you are all very special to me.  Oh, and another thing, if anyone runs away, you will be caught and impaled."

*-Genghis Khan addressing his troops before battle*

"I can't seem to get the top off the ketchup bottle"

*-Max Planck, 1918 Nobel Prize winner and inventor of Quantum Mechanics*

**"Let's talk about something else besides math."**

*-A woman talking to Descartes at a bar*

---

**"Hey, I got an idea.  Why don't we put some kind of oil based mixture on this dry romaine lettuce."**

*-Caesar in the kitchen*

**"Noah, the tigers got loose and ate three species of reptiles, plus they got Billy's leg!"**

*-Noah's first mate*

**"Alright, somebody go get two gnats and let's get out of here."**

*-Noah right before the Ark set sail*

**"Kill him, kill him, kill him, have lunch with him, kill him."**

*-Stalin going over his to do list*

---

**"You know, sometimes I think, Joe, you could of been a great dancer."**

*-Stalin reminiscing in his later years*

"Pass the vodka, pass the meat, pass the potatoes, . . . hey, Sergei, did they wipe out that village today?"

*-Stalin*

---

"Yea, Doc, sometimes I think I'm supposed to feel guilty about these purges but to tell you the truth, I don't. Is that bad?"

*-Stalin on a visit to his therapist*

**"No, I haven't taken Britain.  Did I say I've taken Britain?"**

*-Caesar talking to reporters*

---

**"Throw that man to the lions and pass the grapes."**

*-Caesar*

"Why are we building pyramids when our social programs are so underfunded?"

*-Early Egyptian left wing democrat*

---

"Hey, whose that guy in the grassy knoll?"

*-JFK*

**"How should I know?"**

*-Sherlock Holmes*

**"I wish I had a drachma for every Ottoman I killed with a right sword slash to the neck."**

*-Alexander the Great*

"So this is the Ovating Office."

-Dan Quayle walking into the Oval
office for the first time

"Now tell me again, what does NAFTA
stand for?"

-Al Gore

**"They're fools, I tell you, fools.  Man wasn't meant to fly."**

*-Guy watching the Wright Brothers work on their plane*

---

**"Land, ha, I mean land ho."**

*-Columbus*

"No, no, Queen, I'm not going to another planet."

*-Columbus*

"They want to give us what?"

*-Yasser Arafat*

"Who brought all this cranberry sauce?"

*-Captain of the Mayflower*

"No, let's put the top down."

*-JFK*

"So it was after you talked to the burning bush that you saw the clay tablets at your feet?  Uh huh!"

*-Moses therapist*

"You're not going first, I'm going first."

*-Neil Armstrong to Buzz Aldrin*

**"Sure he's a General, but he can help row the boat."**

*-Two privates talking while Washington was crossing the Potomac.*

---

**"Wait, okay, let me get this straight. You're talking about a mass suicide?"**

*-Some guy at Masadah*

**"Okay, let me ask you, if for instance one of the elephants falls overboard and drowns, should we go ahead and throw the other elephant overboard?"**

*-Noah quizzing his crew*

**"And for God's sake, don't ask him about the way things used to be."**

*-Methuselah's great great grandson taking his kids to see Methuselah*

**"That's right, and then you lay another thin strip of pig next to that one."**

*-Sir Francis Bacon*

**"You know we're not the first.  Lief Ericson was here almost 300 years ago."**

*-A sailor to Columbus*

**"I told you I love you.  Now I suppose you'll want me to count the ways?"**

*-Marital spat at the Browning house*

**"Butter, a sprinkle of salt, a little basil and they're not too bad."**

*-Gregor Mendel conversing with a delegate at the annual pea festival*

**"Tale of ten cities is too much, babe. Maybe two, tops."**

*-Dickens' editor*

---

**"There's a bunch of 'em, but I think we'll make it."**

*-Custer at Little Big Horn*

**"Carlos, you drivin'?  Good.  Juan, did you bring your van?"**

*-Santa Anna working out transportation to the Alamo*

---

**"Oh no, another whale!  Boy, the tuna business is the pits."**

*-Captain Ahab's first job*

**"Tortoise soup again? Didn't we bring any provisions?**

*-Charles Darwin, one week in the Galapagos*

---

**"Listen, you little idiot. I made you what you are. When I say get me coffee, then get me some coffee!"**

*-P.T. Barnum talking to Tom Thumb*

"Sometimes I think, are we really that smart?  I mean we don't have jobs and we wear togas."

*-Plato talking to Aristotle*

"I just want to fly around and clear my head.  I'll be right back."

*-Hess to Hitler*

**"I still can't believe we sold them Alaska."**

*-Yeltsin*

**"Enough with the play dough.  How about a Mr. Potato Head for your birthday?"**

*-Rodan's mother*

"The only drawback of being a viking is that you have to wear this stupid fur hat with horns."

-Lief Ericson

"Man inherently has a universal, . . . hey who spilt coffee on my toga?"

-Plato

"Okay men, before we go pillage and plunder, please remember where you parked your horse."

*-Thor the Viking*

"Hey, shut-up, I'm talking!"

*-Socrates during a speech*

**"Again, Oh my Lord, you shouldn't have!"**

*-Madame Curie when she found out
she won her second Nobel Peace Prize*

---

**"I told him to keep it short."**

*-Mrs. William Henry Harrison talking
about her husband's long inaugural
speech on a cold day where he caught
pneumonia and died*

**"Oh no!  The ocean has risen and we can't get back across the Bering Straits."**

*-An Indian when they tried to go back*

**"Uh Oh!"**

*-Alexander Hamilton after he missed in his duel with Aaron Burr*

**"You'll never be as famous as Columbus!"**

*-Vasco De Gama's mother*

---

**"Scurvy, Schmurvy, don't let it get the best of you men!"**

*-Vasco De Gama dealing with disease and low morale on his ship*

**"Okay, which do you like better? A house divided cannot stand or a house divided is a duplex."**

*-Lincoln talking with his writers*

---

**"Heads, I fight for the South, tails, I fight for the North."**

*-General Lee flipping a coin
to decide his allegiance*

"We can always take it back."

*-Simon Peres talking about giving the Palestineans Jericho and the Gaza Strip*

"Does this mean we can't throw rocks anymore?"

*-A young Palestinean*

"Quit tapping on the table and say what you want to say."

-Mrs. Morse

---

"I would say that my secret to longevity is bran."

-Methuselah

"I am so tired of this armor.  Why don't we try spandex and some padding?"

*-Sir Lancelot*

"I know it's an extra-terrestrial spacecraft.  Just shut-up."

*-Buzz Aldrin to Neil Armstrong, on the moon*

**"Gee, your office is bigger than mine."**

*-Quayle talking to Bush*

**"Now tell me again, which country is the bad guy, North or South Korea?"**

*-Gore talking to Clinton*

**"Do we have to do that ping pong ball thing again?"**

*-Captain Kangaroo*

**"Honey, what did you do with our couch?"**

*-Mrs. Freud*

"Listen, it's really none of my business, but why don't you shoot that 'coon and skin it before you put it back on your head."

*-Doctor treating Davy Crockett for minor bites and scratches*

"Just what am I going to do with all this moldy bread?"

*-Mrs. Alexander Fleming*

"Ivan, why is it that everytime you invite me over for dinner right before you serve it, you ring a bell?"

*-Pavlov's neighbor*

"You're pretty committed to the Hitler guy, huh?"

*-Goering's neighbor*

"Oh no, one crusade to the middle east
is enough for me!"

*-King Richard's neighbor*

"I still can't believe you talked to George
Bush that way."

*-Dan Rather's neighbor*

**"Do you really feel you have to rule the whole world?"**

*-Napoleon's neighbor*

**"So after you take France, you're gonna put your house up for sale?"**

*-Hitler's neighbor*

**"So what was my great, great, great, great, great grandfather like?"**

*-Methuselah's neighbor*

---

**"I guess you'll have to get your glasses adjusted now."**

*-Van Gogh's neighbor*

"No, I disagree, I say it's Mercury, but the wife thinks Venus is the center of the Universe."

-Copernicus' neighbor

---

"Listen, I hate to bother you, but can you tell me another word for tenacious?"

-Roget's neighbor

"So what do philosopher's make an hour?"

*-Socrates' neighbor*

---

"So when are you going back to the Philipines?"

*-MacArthur's neighbor*

"My advice is to just fly domestically!"

*-Amelia Earhart's neighbor*

---

"Okay, show me that trick one more time."

*-Merlin's neighbor*

"Hey, Noah, I hear you're starting a zoo!"

*-Noah's neighbor*

"Hey, Buddy, can you give me a hand with my checking account?"

*-Archimedes' neighbor*

**"So what are you tellin' me?  My great grandfather was a gorilla?"**

*-Darwin's neighbor*

**"Hey, Nostrodamus, you still havin' those wierd dreams?"**

*-Nostrodamus' neighbor*

## If you find any lost quotes, write to:

Lost Quotes
c/o John Marks
P.O. Box 251
Elizabeth Contract Station
Charlotte, N.C.  28204


## For booking information contact:

Terri Beasley
Las Vegas Productions
1-800-285-1377

**HAN HOUSE**
PUBLISHING

1480 Creek Road
Huntingdon Valley, PA 19006